Literacy Strategies Across the Subject Areas
Process-Oriented Blackline Masters for the K-12 Classroom

Karen D. Wood
University of North Carolina, Charlotte

Allyn and Bacon

Boston   London   Toronto   Sydney   Tokyo   Singapore

ISBN 0-205-32658-7

Printed in the United States of America

10 9 8 7 6 5 4 3 2 1   05 04 03 02 01 00

Dedicated, as always, with love to my children: Eric, Ryan, Lauren and Kevin

Table of Contents

Preface

Fellow Educators:

It is a pleasure to introduce a new concept in teacher/student workbooks, *Literacy Strategies Across the Subject Areas*. This book is unique in that it contains *process-oriented* blackline masters for Kindergarten through Grade 12. In typical product-oriented workbooks, worksheets are assigned to students often with little or no guidance or explanation. In *Literacy Strategies Across the Subject Areas*, teachers engage students in strategies to enhance their understanding of various topics under study, modeling, demonstrating and guiding their practice and application along the way. The blackline master serves as a vehicle for aiding this learning process, a place where students can work alone or in pairs to express their new learning.

Each entry in *Literacy Strategies Across the Subject Areas* is presented in the following format:

- ▶ Title
- ▶ Objective
- ▶ Rationale/Description
- ▶ Intended for (appropriate grade and ability levels)
- ▶ Procedures
- ▶ Bibliographic Information
- ▶ Sample Lesson(s)
- ▶ Blackline Master

A strong basis in research and theory underlies the practical applications of this book. A brief description of each of these areas is described next.

Constructivism, Schema Theory and Prior Knowledge:

Reading can be defined as the process of constructing meaning from text. It is a dynamic process that involves a continuous interaction between the reader's prior knowledge and the author's intended message. The importance of prior knowledge for enhancing understanding has been well-established throughout the professional literature (Anderson and Pearson, 1984; Tierney and Pearson, 1994). Our understanding of the significance of prior knowledge in literacy has its roots in schema theory, the notion that individuals develop a cognitive structure in their minds based upon their many and varied experiences (Rumelhart, 1980). Since readers typically come to the reading task with divergent knowledge and abilities, building their background knowledge, getting them to think about what they already know about a topic and then use that information to bridge the gap between what is known and unknown is a time-honored way to improve comprehension and recall. The KWLPlus (pp. 27-31) with its brainstorming phase is excellent for this purpose as is Imagine, Elaborate, Predict and Confirm (IEPC) (pp. 82-86) with its emphasis on creating multi-sensory images and using these visualizations to predict the content of a selection.

Gradual Release Model of Instruction:

The gradual release model of instruction (Pearson, 1985), as with most models of scaffolded instruction, recognizes that effective instruction is more than just assigning, mentioning or telling (Durkin, 1978). Effective instruction means clearly explaining the purposes of the assignment, why and how it is beneficial for the students and then modeling how to engage in the learning strategy. As the chart below shows (Wood, 1998;1999), initially the responsibility rests with the teacher to demonstrate what is expected, "thinking and talking aloud" the processes involved in the learning task and "walking" the students through the procedures. This is typically done in the form of whole class instruction, using classroom examples of the learning material and eliciting input from the students. When the teacher feels the explanation is sufficient, the responsibility can then be released to the students. Many times, it is beneficial to gradually ease into the strategy by allowing students to work in pre-assigned groups. In this way, students can learn from one another while the teacher circulates and monitors to provide assistance. Next, the teacher may suggest that students practice in pairs to reinforce the new learning. Then, when the teacher deems it appropriate, students can be asked to practice their new learning individually. Finally, the new learning is applied to other subject areas. Many of the strategies described in this book involve this gradual release model of instruction. For example, in Story Frames (pp. 97-104), students first learn how to fill out the frames as a class, in small groups and finally independently. Headings divide the procedures by telling the teacher to model/demonstrate/explicate;

engage the students in group practice; engage the students in individual practice; and apply the strategy to other subject areas.

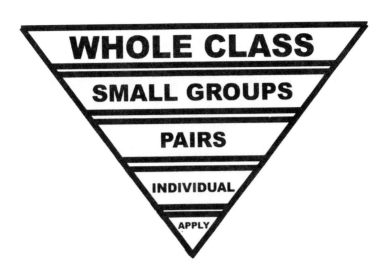

Gradual Release Model of Instruction with Grouping (Wood, 1999)

Metacognition:

Research has shown that metacognition, the awareness and monitoring of one's own thinking processes during learning and problem solving, aids students' understanding and recall (Brown, 1980; Baker and Brown, 1984). One of the ways in which teachers can help students become aware of their thinking is through **"think alouds"** (Davey, 1983). In think alouds, teachers model or describe their own thoughts about a text so that the students can see what is expected and do the same. For example, rather than simply telling students to create an image in their head, teachers can first show students their own thinking by talking about what is going on in their minds. Then the students can practice by sharing their thinking with partners, the class and eventually alone as they engage in self-recitation.

Stages of an instructional lesson:

Another feature of this book is the emphasis on the stages of an instructional lesson. A good lesson, like a good piece of writing, ought to have a beginning, middle and end. Throughout the procedural guidelines of *Literacy Strategies Across the Subject Areas* are the three stages of an instructional lesson: the prereading, reading and postreading stages. The **prereading** stage is the time for explaining the purposes of the assignment, building students' background knowledge, introducing and preteaching significant vocabulary terms, making predictions and helping students' connect the new information with what they already know about a topic as shown in the Story Impressions strategy (pp. 109-112). The **reading stage** is the time for guiding students through the reading of the selection, helping them to focus on the most significant information. This can be done via statements, for example, the Anticipation Guide (pp. 27-30), or through key vocabulary as illustrated in the Possible Sentences strategy (pp. 51-55). The **postreading** stage is when students are asked to return to their original predictions and modify them to coordinate with what was learned as in the Probable Passages strategy (pp. 73-76). It is the time for synthesizing and discussing the new content, extending the new learning through writing or other assignments as in Field Trip Writing Frame (pp. 105-107) or List-Group-Label and Write (pp.7-10).

Collaborative Learning:

There is no doubt that collaborative learning in the form of flexible grouping has the potential to be the individualized instruction of the present and the future (Wood and

Algozzine, 1994). Without some form of grouping and pairing, it is impossible to meet the diverse needs of students in today's classrooms (Tomlinson, 1999). According to Johnson and Johnson (in Brandt, 1987), there is more evidence for the benefits of collaborative learning than any other aspect of education. In a synthesis of the research from many sources (Johnson and Johnson, 1991; Kagan, 1994; Paratore and McCormack, 1997; Slavin, 1995), collaborative learning in the form of flexible grouping has been demonstrated to:

- ▶ Improve peer relationships

- ▶ Increase self-esteem and motivation

- ▶ Aid students in accepting diversity

- ▶ Improve achievement scores

- ▶ Improve performance in all subject areas

- ▶ Improve performance of all ability levels

- ▶ Decrease reliance on the teacher

In *Literacy Strategies Across the Subject Areas*, the use of group and paired interaction is suggested in almost every strategy described. For example, students talk over their ideas about how to solve a problem or undertake a task in Think Pair Share (pp. 81-83). In Talking Drawings (pp. 1-5), they share their artistic interpretations of topics with a partner and in the Collaborative Listening-Viewing Guide CLVG (pp. 37-39), they engage in whole class, small group, paired and individual activities in response to demonstrations, videos, field trips, etc.

xi

Diverse Learners:

Many of the strategies are listed as being particularly effective for students who need additional language support. Teachers will find these strategies very beneficial to students for whom English is a second language as well as students with other diverse needs. For example, Paired Reading for Fluency (pp. 65-67) is a repeated reading strategy that enables partners to practice reading short passages (preferably related to topics under study) until "fluency," smoothness of reading, is attained. Other strategies recommend small, heterogeneous groups be used to ensure that students of all ability levels feel included within the classroom community. In Exchange-Compare Writing (pp. 57-60), students work in groups to assist one another, model reading and writing processes and receive individual attention as needed from the teacher.

It is my hope that *Literacy Strategies Across the Subject Areas* will be a practical resource for classroom teachers of all grade levels and subject areas, curriculum coordinators, administrators and teacher educators and anyone else charged with providing staff development training. Here's to a new millennium of improved teaching and learning!

Sincerely,

References

Anderson, R. C. & Pearson, P. D. (1984) A schema-theoretic view of basic process in reading comprehension. In P. D. Pearson (Ed.) *Handbook of reading research* (pp. 255-291). New York: Longman.

Baker, L. & Brown, A. L. (1984) Metacognitive skills in reading. In P. D. Pearson (Ed.) *Handbook of reading research* (pp. 353-394). New York: Longman.

Brandt, R. (1987) On cooperation in schools: A conversation with David and Roger Johnson. *Educational Leadership*, 45 (3), 14-19.

Brown, A. L. (1980) Metacognitive development and reading. In R. J. Spiro, B. C. Bruce, & W. F. Brewer (Eds.), *Theoretical issues in reading comprehension* (pp. 453-481). Hillsdale, NJ: Lawrence Erlbaum.

Davey, B. (1983). Think-aloud—modeling the cognitive processes of reading comprehension. *Journal of Reading* 27(1), pp. 44-47.

Durkin, D. (1978) What classroom observations reveal about reading comprehension instruction. *Reading Research Quarterly*, 14(4), 481-533.

Johnson, D. W. & Johnson., R. T. (1991) *Learning together and alone* (3rd ed.) Boston, MA: Allyn and Bacon.

Kagan, S. (1994) *Cooperative learning*. San Juan, CA: Kagan Cooperative Learning.

Parratore, J. R. & McCormack, R. L., Editors (1997) Peer talk in the classroom: Learning from research. Newark, DE: International Reading Association.

Pearson, P. D. (1985) Changing the face of reading comprehension instruction. *The Reading Teacher*, 38, 724-738.

Rumelhart, D. E. (1980) Schemata: The building blocks of cognition. In R. J. Spiro et al. (Eds.) *Theoretical issues in reading comprehension* (pp. 33-58). Hillsdale, NJ: Lawrence Erlbaum.

Tomlinson, C. A. (1999) *The differentiated classroom: Responding to the needs of all learners*. Alexandria, VA: Association for Supervision and Curriculum Development.

Slavin. R. (1995) *Cooperative learning* (2nd ed.) Needham Heights, MA: Allyn and Bacon.

Tierney, R. J. & Pearson, P. D. (1994) Learning to learn from text: A framework for improving classroom practice. In R. B. Ruddell, M. R. Ruddell & H. Singer (Eds.) *Theoretical models and processes of reading* (4th ed. pp. 496-513). Newark, DE: International Reading Association.

Wood, K. D. (1999) Including diverse learners in the classroom community. Keynote address for the Eastern Regional Conference of the International Reading Association. Dover, Delaware.

Wood, K. D. and Algozzine, B., Editors (1994) *Teaching reading to high risk learners: An integrated approach*. Boston: Allyn and Bacon.

Talking Drawings

Objective: To promote the use of prior knowledge in the improvement of recall and comprehension.

Rationale/Description: Creating mental images before and after the reading of a selection to help students connect what is known about a topic with what is to be newly learned is a proven way to enhance students' understanding and recall. "Talking Drawings" is a strategy in which students draw pictures of their mental images of a topic, character or event before reading a selection, talking about and analyzing the drawings with a partner. After reading the selection, the students construct another drawing that depicts their newly learned knowledge.

Intended for: Elementary, intermediate, middle and secondary and students who need additional support.

Procedures:

Prereading Stage

Step One: Ask students to close their eyes and imagine the topic, event or character to be studied. Then tell them to open their eyes and draw what they saw in their minds.

Step Two: Have the students share their drawings with at least two other students. Here they can talk about and analyze why they depicted the topic as they did.

Step Three: Then the students can share their thinking and drawings with the whole class, explaining personal experiences and sources of information that helped them in their drawings. From the whole class discussion, a concept map or cluster of information can be written on the board, reflecting the contributions of the class.

Reading Stage

Step Four: Have the students open their textbooks to the appropriate selection or distribute the relevant reading material and have them read the passage with their drawings in mind.

Postreading Stage

Step Five: Engage in a small group or whole class discussion of the article and then ask the students to develop a new drawing or change the existing one to correspond with the new information.

Step Six: Have the students share and compare their before and after drawings with partners or group members, discussing the reasons for the changes made. Students can be encouraged to return to the selection to read aloud specific parts in the passage that support the changes they made.

Step Seven: An optional step is to have the students write what they have changed from drawing one to drawing number two.

Step Eight: The new learning can be extended by having the students further research related areas of the topic on the internet or through other available sources.

McConnell, S. (1992/3). Talking drawings: A strategy for assisting learners. *Journal of Reading, 36* (4), 260-269.

Talking Drawings Sample Narrative Lesson

1. **Close your eyes and think about <u>a wolf</u>. Now, open your eyes draw what you saw.**

2. **Read/Listen to the selection, _Wolf_ by Becky Bloom, then draw a second picture to show what you learned.**

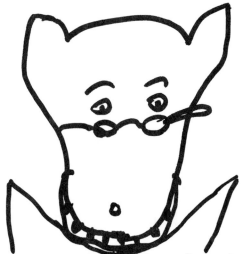

3. **In the space below, tell what you have changed about your before and after pictures.**

<u>The wolf in this story isn't like the one in Little Red Riding Hood. He starts off mean and tries to scare everyone. Then, he watches the cow, pig and duck love to read. He wants to impress his friends. So, he decides he better learn to read, too.</u>

Talking Drawings Sample Expository Lesson

1. **Close your eyes and think about <u>volcanoes</u>. Now, open your eyes draw what you saw.**

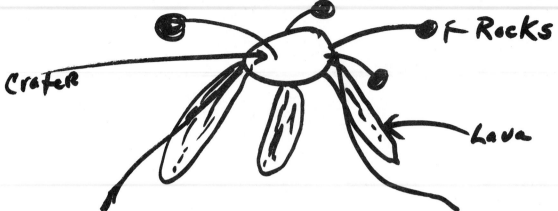

2. **Read your selection on "<u>Volcanoes" from Chapter 12</u> then draw a second picture to show what you learned.**

3. **In the space below, tell what you have changed about your before and after pictures.**

   At first, I only drew the mountain and the lava coming down the sides. From our textbook and the video, I learned that there is a magma chamber inside that causes the eruption to flow through the pipe and out the caldera, the huge opening at the top. There is a river of lava that flows down the side of the mountain. Ash and volcanic bombs can be seen around the volcano.

Talking Drawings Form

1. Close your eyes and think about _____. Now, open your eyes draw what you saw.

2. Read your selection _____ then draw a second picture to show what you learned.

3. In the space below, tell what you have changed about your before and after pictures.

_____

_____

_____

_____

_____

Paired Comprehension and Retelling

Objective: To help students practice retelling with partners as a means of increasing comprehension.

Rationale/Description: Retelling, the ability to put information in one's own word, is a significant way to evaluate and reinforce understanding. Getting students to retell the contents of a narrative or expository passage to a partner is an excellent means of enhancing comprehension and recall.

Intended for: Elementary, middle, secondary and students who need additional support.

Procedures:

Modeling Stage

> **Step One:** Decide upon the material to be used to model and then practice the act of retelling. It is often best to use material that is familiar and used in the classroom.

> **Step Two:** Explain to the students that one of the best ways to help them remember what they read is to recite the content, using their own language as much as possible. Tell them that they are going to learn a strategy to help them know how to retell information.

> **Step Three:** Display the retelling form on an overhead projector. Then, read aloud a brief passage to the class and put the information in your own words. (Concentrate on either narrative or expository material for the introductory and practice sessions, then introduce the other after sufficient practice is achieved.) Focus on the characters, setting and events of the story for fiction or on the recall of the main idea and details for non-fiction. Model how to elaborate, imagine and relate content to prior experiences.

> **Step Four:** Ask the class to join you in evaluating the retelling, marking the responses on the transparency.

Guided Practice

> **Step Five:** Have students open their books to a specified passage or hand out a passage for practice. Assign students to partners and have them whisper read the passage together, read to one another or read the selection silently.

> **Step Six:** Encourage partners to add to and embellish each other's retelling with analogies, anecdotes and questions about the topic.

11

Step Seven: As the partners work together to write their brief retellings in the space provided, monitor the students to evaluate and provide assistance as needed.

Independent Practice

Step Eight: Have students practice individually, putting information in their own words after reading both with and later without the form.

Step Nine: Tell the class to apply the strategy of retelling, either mentally or in writing, when they read and study other subjects.

Adapted from Koskinen, P.S., Gambrell, L. G., Kapinus, B. & Heathington, B. (1988) Retelling: A strategy for enhancing students' reading comprehension. *The Reading Teacher, 41(9* 892-96.

Personal Vocabulary Journal

Objective: To enable students to self select their own vocabulary terms to develop and increase their vocabulary knowledge.

Rationale/Description: Most vocabulary terms learned by students are determined by the teacher, usually through commercially-prepared materials and textbooks. Consequently, students do not get the opportunity to learn vocabulary of their own choosing, based on their individual interests. The "Personal Vocabulary Journal" can be used by teachers at all grade levels and subject areas to help focus students' attention on new words of interest throughout their daily life at home or at school.

Intended for: Students of all grade levels, ability levels and subject areas.

Procedures:

> **Step One:** Ask the students if they ever heard or read a word in or out of class and wondered what it meant. Also, inquire if they would like to have the opportunity to choose their own words to study instead of having the teacher decide which words are most important.

> **Step Two:** Display a blank vocabulary form either via a handout or an overhead projector or both. Tell the students that they will use this form to record one or two (or more) vocabulary terms of interest to them or that relate to the particular unit of study.

> **Step Three:** Demonstrate a sample entry by "thinking aloud" the process students would undergo to select and record their entries. Enlist the participation of the class whenever possible.

> **Step Four:** Make copies of the personal vocabulary journal master that has two entries per page and distribute to the class. Explain that they may be asked to keep a vocabulary journal for other subjects as well. Also, explain that for language arts class, they may be asked to choose any word encountered that interests them, not necessarily related to a topic studied in class.

> **Step Five:** (Discussion Option) Students can be assigned to small groups of five to eight students to share their words of choice from their vocabulary journals. When appropriate, they may be asked to "act out" their words or make a drawing to depict its meaning.

Step Six: (Assessment Option) Students may be asked to select two or three words or more from their personal vocabulary collection for the weekly or unit vocabulary test/quiz. These terms can be submitted to the teacher for assessment purposes.

Wood, K. D. (1994). Practical strategies for improving instruction. Columbus, OH: National Middle School Association.

Personal Vocabulary Collection

My new word is __squall__

It is related to __our science unit on "weather"__

I found it __on the weather station on TV__

The specific context is __New Yorkers were surprised with a thick squall early this morning. No precipitation is expected tomorrow, however.__

I think it means __rain storm__

The appropriate dictionary definition is __a sudden gust of wind; a black squall has dark clouds; a thick squall has hail or sleet.__

It reminds me of __the word "squall" used in our Language Arts story which meant "to scream".__

My sentence is: __The black squall scared the young children as they played ball in the street.__

Personal Vocabulary Collection

My new word is _____

It is related to _____

I found it _____

The specific context is

_____

_____

_____

I think it means _____

The appropriate dictionary definition is _____

_____

_____

It reminds me of _____

_____

_____

My sentence is _____

_____

_____

_____

_____

Retelling Form

Name _____ **Date** _____

I listened to _____.

Choose one or more things your partner did well:

Fiction   **My partner told about:**

_____ The characters.

_____ The setting.

_____ The events in the story.

_____ The beginning.

_____ The ending.

Non-fiction   **My partner told about:**

_____ The main ideas.

_____ The details.

With the aid of your partner, retell the selection in your own words in the space below.

_____

_____

_____

_____

_____

_____

Semantic Feature Analysis

Objective: To help fine-tune students' understanding of key vocabulary and concepts.

Rationale/Description: This strategy uses a matrix to help students see the common elements and differences among key concepts under study. Questioning and writing can be used to help further solidify their understanding of the key terms.

Intended for: Elementary, Intermediate, Middle, and Secondary students

Procedures:

> **Step One:** Select a category based on a topic under study in which at least two items are similar. For example, choose animals, elements, planets, explorers, scientific classes, words with similar meanings, historical or literary characters, etc.

> **Step Two:** Write or type the features of the category chosen across the top of the matrix provided.

> **Step Three:** Write or type the terms or concepts on the left-hand side of the matrix.

> **Step Four:** Make an overhead transparency of the matrix and display it on an overhead projector. Explain to the students that examining the terms this way will help them further understand the concepts.

> **Step Five:** Model one or two examples as a class to explicate the process. Then, guide the students through the matrix as a whole class, in groups or pairs, or individually by having them indicate with a plus (+) if an item contains a feature of minus (-) if it does not.

> **Step Six:** Help the students make some generalizations about the concepts by guiding them with specific questions. For example, "How is _____ different from or similar to _____?" or "Which is the longest... hottest... smallest... etc.?"

> **Step Seven:** An optional step is to have students write down either in list or paragraph form some key concepts they have learned from engaging in this strategy.

Johnson, D. D. & Pearson, P. D. (1984). *Teaching reading vocabulary* (2nd ed.). New York: Holt, Rinehart, and Winston.

Semantic Feature Analysis
Geography/Economics

Products of the Thirteen Colonies

	Grain	Tobacco	Iron	Cattle	Furs	Lumber	Naval Supplies
Connecticut	-	-	+	+	-	-	-
Massachusetts	+	-	+	+	-	-	+
New Hampshire	-	-	-	-	+	-	+
Rhode Island	-	-	+	-	-	-	-
Delaware	-	+	-	-	-	-	-
Maryland	-	+	-	+	-	-	-
New Jersey	-	-	+	-	-	-	-
New York	+	-	+	+	+	+	-
Pennsylvania	+	-	+	+	+	+	-
Georgia	-	-	-	-	+	-	-
North Carolina	+	+	-	+	+	+	+
South Carolina	+	-	-	-	-	+	+
Virginia	+	+	-	-	+	-	-

Summary

What conclusions can you draw by studying the information on the chart?

These thirteen colonies produced many types of goods. Furs were gathered in states from north to south, but cattle was more common in the north than the south. Naval supplies were made only in states near the coast, and tobacco was grown mostly in the Middle States.

Semantic Feature Analysis
Geography/Economics

Products of the Thirteen Colonies

	Grain	Tobacco	Iron	Cattle	Furs	Lumber	Naval Supplies
New England Colonies (Connecticut, Massachusetts, New Hampshire, Rhode Island)	+	-	+	+	+	-	-
Middle Colonies (Delaware, Maryland, New Jersey, New York, Pennsylvania)	+	+	+	+	+	+	-
Southern Colonies (Georgia, North Carolina, South Carolina, Virginia)	+	+	-	+	+	+	+

Summary

What conclusions can you draw by studying the information on the chart?

These thirteen colonies produced many types of goods. Furs were gathered in states from north to south, but cattle was more common in the north than the south. Naval supplies were made only in states near the coast and tobacco was grown mostly in the Middle States.

Semantic Feature Analysis

Summary

What conclusions can you draw by studying the information on the chart?

Language Charts

Rationale/Description: A language chart is a matrix to enable students to recall and save their ideas about literature selections they have read (usually on related topics or themes). Students, with the help of the teacher, students rely on the chart to help them recall other stories in a unit and to notice similarities and differences. The language chart is most effective when comparing two or more books that share some common element (such as theme, topic, genre, author/illustrator), although it can be used after the reading of a single selection to help students recap the events and story line.

Intended for: Elementary, intermediate, middle and secondary

Procedures:

Step One: The teacher may choose to use the blank language chart included here or it can be constructed from a large piece of butcher paper ruled into a matrix. Present the blank form via an overhead projector and explain its purpose as a means of organizing their ideas about literature selections read.

Step Two: Write in the titles and authors of the selections under study. At this point, the teacher may also include the questions along the top of the matrix to be considered or elicit questions from the students.

Step Three: Students and teacher share their thinking about the questions posed and how the responses are similar or different for each story read. These responses are recorded in the appropriate places on the language chart.

Options:

▸ The language charts for each theme under study can be enlarged, decorated with children's artwork and comments and displayed in the classroom.

▸ Students can work as a whole class or they can be divided into groups to fill in information on group copies of the language chart.

▸ Teachers can use response journals in combination with language charts by asking students to take a few minutes immediately after reading a story to record their personal reflections. (For emergent readers, this may take the form of illustrations, whereas for more experienced readers and writers, the responses may be more extensive.) Then, the teachers can ask students to volunteer their responses each day as a stimulus for group discussion. Finally, after a thorough exploration of their thinking and talking, the collective responses are recorded on the language chart.

Roser, N. L., Hoffman, J. V., Labbo, L. D. and Farest, C. (1992) Language charts: A record of story time talk. *Language Arts, 69,* 44-52.

Excerpt from a Language Chart

Title/Author/Type	Characters	Main Problem(s)/Issue(s)/Event(s)	How did their relationship change?	What was learned?
The Cay Theodore Taylor (Adventure)	Phillip, 11 years old, is shipwrecked with Timothy, a West Indian.	Phillip doesn't trust Timothy at first and isn't nice to him.	Timothy helps Phillip when he goes blind.	That we are all human beings and deserve respect.
Crash Jerry Spinelli (Sports)	Crash Coogan, a 7th grade football star; Mike, his friend and a prankster; Webb, a nerd who is picked on.	(1) Crash's grandfather has a stroke. (2) Mike and Crash pick on Webb for being different.	Webb gives Crash a present to help cure his sick grandfather and Crash helps Webb win the race.	That people who are different can be great friends.
Shiloh	Marty Preston, an 11 year-old; Shiloh, a dog nobody wants; Judd, the dog's mean owner.	Marty finds a mistreated beagle pup and hides it in the woods, away from his parents.	Marty offers to work for Judd so that he may keep the dog; he also agrees to keep quiet about Judd's deer hunting.	That lying only leads to more problems, but it is important to help animals and people.

Language Chart

Anticipation Guide

Objective: To help stimulate discussion and critical thinking to enable students to better understand expository and narrative material.

Rationale/Description: The Anticipation Guide (variations may be called reasoning, prediction or reaction guides) is a series of teacher-generated statements that help elicit students' prior knowledge and reveal possible misconceptions about certain key concepts before reading a selection. Variations may be called reasoning, prediction or reaction guides. When they use the statements to guide their reading, students respond after reading to see if they have changed their mind or broadened their view.

Intended for: Elementary, Intermediate, Middle and Secondary level.

Procedures:

Teacher Preparation Stage

Decide on a story, textbook selection, newspaper article or any other material to be studied and note the key concepts and lesson objectives. Develop approximately five to ten statements, not questions, that reflect these key concepts. Make certain that the statements are sufficiently general and likely stimulate students' thinking. Type or write the statements on the blank anticipation guide form provided and run copies for the students.

Prereading Stage

Step One: Display the guide on an overhead projector and introduce it as a means of improving students' understanding by helping them bring all they know and can predict about a topic before reading.

Step Two: Tell them to take turns reading each of the statements with their partner indicating if they agree or disagree with the content. They do not have to agree with each other, but it is essential that they substantiate their answers.

Step Three: You may choose to engage in a whole class discussion of the answers in order to ascertain their level of prior knowledge or degree of misconceptions about the topic. Explain to the students that, at this point, they are free to share their thinking and predictions and that no one will be put on the spot.

Reading Stage

Step Four: Have the students read, listen to or view the related material using the statements as their guide to the key concepts in the selection.

     Step Five: After reading the selection, have the students respond as a class, individually, in pairs or small groups to indicate if they agree or disagree with each statement now that they have read the entire selection. It is important that students be required to discuss the reasons behind their answers, even indicating where in the text they located the answer.

Readence, J. E., Bean, T. W. & Baldwin, R. S. (1989). *Content area reading: An integrated approach.* Dubuque, IA: Kendall-Hunt.

Anticipation Guide

Ducks Don't Get Wet
Augusta Goldin

Before   **After**

_____   _____   1. Bird and duck feathers are waterproof.

_____   _____   2. You can easily mix oil and water together.

_____   _____   3. Most ducks don't dive very deeply.

_____   _____   4. Ducks can swim the length of a city block.

_____   _____   5. Ducks can fly as fast as an automobile.

_____   _____   6. When ducks are hungry, they fly south.

Anticipation Guide for _____

Name_____   Partner_____

Before   **After**

_____   _____   1._____
                                _____

_____   _____   2._____
                                _____

_____   _____   3._____
                                _____

_____   _____   4._____
                                _____

_____   _____   5._____
                                _____

_____   _____   6._____
                                _____

_____   _____   7._____
                                _____

_____   _____   8._____
                                _____

_____   _____   9._____
                                _____

_____   _____   10._____
                                _____

30

Collaborative Listening—Viewing Guide (CLVG)

Objective: To help students learn from visual information.

Rationale/Description: The collaborative listening-viewing guide (CLVG) is a lesson framework to help students learn from information observed and/or heard. It can be used to manage and organize content learned from experiments, demonstrations, lectures, information on field trips or videotapes.

Intended for: Elementary, intermediate, middle and secondary and students who need additional support.

Procedures:

Step One: *Preview/review information.* In this introductory phase, give an overview of the topic, preteach significant terms if needed and/or elicit the students' background knowledge on the topic. This information can be organized on the board in the form of a semantic map.

Step Two: *Record individually.* Instruct the class to write down significant ideas, concepts, phrases, etc. on the left-hand side of their paper. Students should be instructed to be brief and use abbreviations as needed. Notes should be recorded in sequential order.

Step Three: *Elaborate in Small Groups.* After viewing the video, have the students get in groups to elaborate on their individual notes (it is best if these heterogeneous groups are established beforehand). Here, they can recall details, extend ideas, add personal anecdotes, etc. Then they record this information on the right hand side of their forms.

Step Four: *Synthesize with Whole Class.* Tell the students to contribute what they learned from their group recollections and then record their responses on the board, chart paper or a transparency. This information can then be reorganized as a map, chart or outline form, if appropriate.

Step Five: *Extend in pairs.* An optional step is to have students work in pairs to a) design a project related to the topic, b) compose a paragraph synthesizing some of the information, c) develop a chart or map of the key concepts, d) write a play or a skit, or e) research an aspect of the topic in more detail.

Wood, K. D. (1994) *Practical strategies for improving instruction.* Columbus, OH: National Middle School Association.

Excerpt from a
Collaborative Listening/Viewing Guide

Class <u>Miss Maye</u>   Date <u>Jan. 28, 1999</u>   Topic <u>War of 1812</u>

Student's Name __<u>Ryan</u>__   Group Members __<u>Tonya</u>__

Partner <u>Joshua</u>___   _____<u>Miguel</u>_____

We know that: - that in early 1800's President Jefferson
                       didn't want war
                 - that trade was important to us

My Notes	Our Group's Notes
- Britain took our soldiers	- Captured our ships and men to fight in the war with France. - Said they were British citizens who deserted.
- War hogs wanted war	- War Hawks and other Americans wanted war but some who trade with Britain weren't too happy. - President Madison gets Congress to declare war June 18, 1812.
- Indians sided with the British	- Out west, Tecumseh helped British take Detroit and Chicago - In east they burned the White House. Frances
- Frances Scott Key wrote anthem	Scott Key wrote a poem that was set to music as our national anthem while in prison. - Also burned other government buildings. - In south, General Jackson led Americans to
- Andrew Jackson fought Americans war	defeat Britain. They lost over 1900 soldiers in the Battle of New Orleans

We learned that: British leaves us alone, American trade improves, new
                        factories started.

We will find out: More about President Jackson (Josh and Ryan)
                        Tecumseh

38

Listening/Viewing Guide

Class _____   **Date** _____   **Topic** _____

Student's Name _____   **Group Members** _____

Partner _____   _____

We know that:

My Notes	Our Group's Notes

We learned that:

We will find out:

Multiple Source Research

Objective: To give students practice and instruction in using multiple information sources in their writing.

Rationale/Description: In our information-laden society, it is imperative that students be able to locate, interpret and synthesize information from a number of sources (e.g. the internet, email interviews, public television broadcasts and trade books, etc.). The procedures that follow show how flexible grouping, along with the gradual release model of instruction, can be used to teach students how to synthesize information from multiple sources.

Intended for: Upper elementary, Intermediate, Middle and Secondary Levels

Procedures:

Preparation/Modeling Phase (Whole Class)

Step One: Begin by displaying at least one sample, finished product (research paper or shorter research composition) via an overhead projector or a handout and walk the students through the organization and elements reflected in the composition. It can also be helpful to show examples of research reports that contain negative elements (e.g. one or two sources, copying from a source, lack of coherence, etc.).

StepTwo: Before the actual writing of the paper, engage the class (possibly with the aid of the school media specialist) in several hands-on demonstrations on where to find and how to use varied sources. It may also be necessary to "talk aloud," while engaging the class in how to paraphrase key concepts.

Guided Practice (Small Groups)

Step Three: Assign students to heterogeneous groups of four to six and allow them to physically group their desks together for the purpose of undertaking their next assignment.

Step Four: Either give them the topic(s) under study or have the groups select the unit-related topic of their choice. Hand out the "multiple source research form" to each student and explain its use for recording information from varied sources. Help them to get into the habit of writing down the reference information for each source used, in preparation for developing a bibliography at the end of the paper.

Step Five: Have the students within each group decide who will go to which Source for the information. For example, a student proficient in internet use might select that source, whereas an avid reader might feel more knowledgeable looking at trade books. Students with limited English proficiency or other struggling learners may be paired with another group member to assist with the research process. Flexible grouping in this instance, takes the form of "grouping within the group" to facilitate learning.

Step Six: After allowing the necessary time either in class, the media center or at home to gather the preliminary information, the groups get together to discuss their findings and decide how the final product will proceed. (The headings in sample composition show characteristics, locations, consequences of volcanoes, for example.)

Step Seven: Group members can then be asked to contribute what they found related to the pre-selected sub-areas.

Step Eight: Students can alternate the role of "recorder" or "typist" for each section of the report, carefully writing down related information and the source from which it came. Students may be taught to include their source(s) in parentheses at the end of the related paragraph or sentence as well as being taught to include a reference list.

Step Nine: Then, as is the case in many writing group arrangements, students can assume various roles such as "proofreader," "editor" or "final draft writer" to complete the finished product.

Guided Practice (Pairs)
Step Ten: After at least one opportunity to research and write in small groups as described previously, the teacher may feel that the students are able to engage in this process with the aid of a partner of similar ability level. The subsequent, subject-related research assignment will then be undertaken by two students rather than a group of five or six.

Individual Practice
Step Eleven: After it is deemed that a sufficient number of guided practice sessions have been provided, the students should be allowed to research a topic, using multiple sources independently.

Wood, K. D. (1998) Flexible grouping and information literacy: A model of direct instruction. *North Carolina Middle Schools Association Journal, 19* (2), 1-5.

Sample Collaborative Report Using Multiple Sources
Volcanoes

Parts of Volcanoes

A volcano is an opening in the earth's crust. Gas and rock come from inside the earth onto the surface. The rock is usually very hot. It is called molten, which means "melted." Scientists also call this molten rock "magma." When a volcano erupts, lava flows down the sides of the volcano. In the video, it looked like a snake moving fast down the mountain. The lava has a temperature of about 2,000 degrees. (**CD ROM:** Explorapedia; **VIDEO:** Hill of Fire, Reading Rainbow)

Facts about Volcanoes

An active volcano is when the volcano could erupt again. A volcano that is between eruptions is said to be dormant. Volcanoes are called extinct if they have stopped erupting altogether. There are about 1500 active volcanoes. (**BOOK:** Volcanoes of the World) Another source said that there are about 850 active volcanoes in the world. (**CD ROM:** Explorapedia)

When a volcano erupts after being dormant for a long time, the eruption is often violent. Mount St. Helen erupted in 1980 more than 120 years after its last eruption. The force of the eruption blew the top clear off the mountain!
(**WEBSITE:** Volcanoworld.http://volcano.und.novak.educ)

Kilauea (in Hawaii) is thought to be the world's most active volcano. It has been continually erupting since 1983. Mauna Loa is the largest volcano in the world.
(**WEBSITE:** Volcanoworld)

What Volcanoes Are Really Like

You can even take vacations in volcanoes. They have a drive-in volcano in the Caribbean where you can stay in your car and see the sights. (**TV BROADCAST:** Volcano Hot Spots, CBS News, June 2, 1997)

There is a great website all about volcanoes called Volcanoworld. You can look at other student's homepages and make one, too. Also, you can take virtual reality tours of volcano sites.

Kevin=TV/PBS	Yen-Yi=Internet
Lauren=Books	Michael=Software/Video

From: Wood, K.D. (1998). Flexible and Information Literacy: A Model of Direct Instruction. *North Carolina Middle School Association Journal, 19* (2), 1-5. Reprinted with permission.

Multiple Source Research Form

Name(s): __Yen Yi/Michael__ Group Members: __Kevin, Lauren__

Our research topic is _____Volcanoes_____

I/we am/are searching the following sources: internet; videos; newspapers/magazines; encyclopedias; email interviews; software; public TV; trade books; phone/person to person interviews; biographies; other_____.

Subtopic 1: __violent eruptions occur when a volcano has been dormant a long time 120 years since last eruption. Mt. St. Helens force blew the top off the mountain__
Reference Information: __Volcanoworld   http://volcano.und.novak.edu__

Subtopic 2: __Lava has a temperature 2000 degrees Looks like a snake moving down a mountain.   Molten   means   melted__
Reference Information: __"Hill of Fire" Reading Rainbow Video__

Subtopic 3: __largest volcano is Mauna Loa   Kilauea is most active volcano - erupting since 1983   (Hawaii)__
Reference Information: __Volcanoworld__

Subtopic 4: __850 active volcanoes   Molten rock is called magma__

Reference Information: __CDROM: Explorapedia__

48

Multiple Source Research Form

Name:_____GroupMembers_____

_____

Our research topic is _____

I am searching the following sources: internet; videos; newspapers/magazines; encyclopedias; email interviews; software; public TV; trade books; phone/person to person interviews; biographies; other_____.

Reference Information:_____

Subtopic1:_____
_____
_____
_____
_____
_____

Reference Information: _____

Subtopic 2:_____
_____
_____
_____
_____
_____

Reference Information:_____

Subtopic 3:_____
_____
_____
_____
_____
_____

Reference Information:_____

Subtopic 4:_____
_____
_____
_____
_____
_____

Reference Information: _____

Possible Sentences

Objective: To help reinforce the understanding and recall of key concepts.

Rationale/Description: Possible Sentences provides direct instruction on the unfamiliar vocabulary of a reading selection by drawing on students' existing knowledge of the new vocabulary. The main purpose of this strategy is to assist students to determine independently the meanings and relationships of new words by using the context of the reading selection. Since students use their prior knowledge to predict relationships among new vocabulary items, their motivation to read the assignment is increased, and a mental set is developed for reading the new material.

Procedures:

Step One: Select key vocabulary terms from a content area textbook selection, trade book, short story, basal reader or newspaper article to be read (approximately 6-8 for beginning or struggling readers and 10-15 for average and above readers). These terms should reflect the major concepts in the selection and may include a combination of new, somewhat familiar and very familiar terms.

Prereading Stage
Step Two: Visually display the key terms of the selection on the chalkboard, poster paper, or the overhead projector and have the students pronounce each term after the teacher. (The blank form included can be used to display the terms via transparency and make copies for students as well.)

Step Three: Ask the students to compose a sentence that they think may <u>possibly</u> appear in the selection to be read, that uses two of these vocabulary words. (It is important to emphasize that the sentences not be personal e.g. "I know someone that pollutes the environment." Instead, they should be similar in style and format to the selection under study. The teacher may want to model an example. Write each sentence on the board or overhead exactly as dictated by the students, even though the information may be inaccurate. Continue this procedure until the students are unable to produce any more sentences.

Reading Stage
Step Four: Tell the students that they are to read the assigned selection with these sentences as their guides. They are to read to either confirm or refute the information reflected in the sentences. Using the blank form, have the students write <u>T</u> if they believe the sentence is true, <u>F</u> if they believe it is false, and <u>DK</u> if they do not know whether a sentence is true or false. It is not necessary for them to copy these sentences on their paper, since the sentences may not be true.

Postreading Stage

Step Five: As an oral or written activity(dependent on time constraints) for the whole class or for groups, have students make the necessary revisions in the existing sentences to comply with the selection they read, that is, to rewrite the sentences to make them true. Should disagreements emerge, have the students refer to the text.

Step Six: After the final modifications have been completed, the teacher may have the students record the sentences on the blank form to assist them later with the vocabulary and key concepts under study.

Step Seven (Optional): Have the students go back to the key concepts after the exercise and review meanings.

Moore, D. W., Moore, S. A. (1986) Possible sentences. In *Reading in the content areas: Improving classroom instruction* 2nd edition, edited by E. K. Dishner, T. W. Bean, J. E. Readence and D. W. Moore. Dubuque, IA: Kendall/Hunt.

Possible Sentences Sample Lesson
Science: Topic "Pollution"

1. Key Concepts

environment

pollution

exhaust

custodians

chlorine

carbon monoxide

sulphur

sanitary landfills

billboard

electricity

smog

recycling

2.   Student-generated "possible sentences" (Before Reading) and Postreading reactions – T,F,DK-Don't Know

__ 1.   Pollution is dangerous to our health.

__ 2.   Electricity is one way to get rid of pollution in the environment.

__ 3.   Too much chlorine in the air is bad for your lungs.

__ 4.   The smog makes it hard to breathe.

__ 5.   Billboards often say not to pollute.

__ 6.   Custodians work in schools to keep them clean.

__ 7.   The exhaust from a car is called carbon monoxide.

__ 8.   Too much recycling causes pollution.

__ 9.   Sulfur is caused by factory pollution.

3.   Modified sentences

___1.   Pollution is dangerous to our health.

___2.   We can help stop pollution by using electricity wisely.

___3.   Water treated with chlorine, which kills bacteria, makes it safe to drink.

___4.   Gases, smoke and moisture form smog, which makes it hard for us to see distances.

___5.   Billboards and junkyards spoil the natural beauty of the land.

___6.   Custodians work in schools, hospitals and other buildings to keep them clean.

___7.   The exhaust from a car is called carbon monoxide and is one of the most dangerous pollutants.

___8.   Paper, glass and metal can be collected for recycling, using over again.

___9.   Sulfur is a pollutant caused by nature and sometimes found in spring water. It makes water unhealthful to drink and makes it smell bad.

Possible Sentences Sample Lesson
Reading/Language Arts

<u>Freckle Juice</u> Judy Blume

1. **Key concepts**

Refrigerator	Mayonnaise	Greenish
Gulped	Absolutely	Moaned
Stomach	Awful	Mistake
Vinegar	Decorated	Probably
Ketchup	Andrew Marcus	

2. **Student generated "possible sentences" (Before reading) and Postreading reactions -T,F,DK-Don't Know**

   ___1. Andrew Marcus probably put vinegar in the formula by mistake.

   ___2. He put the secret formula in the refrigerator to keep the mayonnaise cold.

   ___3. The freckle juice he gulped was greenish in color.

   ___4. The recipe for freckle juice contained vinegar, ketchup and mayonnaise.

   ___5. Andrew Marcus moaned after drinking the juice.

   ___6. The juice he put in his stomach tasted absolutely awful.

   ___7. Jars of mayonnaise and ketchup decorated the refrigerator shelves.

3. **Modified Sentences**

   ___1. Andrew Marcus dropped a lemon seed in the formula by mistake.

   ___2. He found everything on the shelves except the lemon and onion that were in the refrigerator.

   ___3. Andrew turned greenish and felt very sick.

   ___4. The recipe for freckle juice contained vinegar, ketchup and mayonnaise as well as lemon, pepper, salt, olive oil, onion, grape juice and mustard.

   ___5. Andrew Marcus moaned after drinking the juice.

   ___6. The juice he put in his stomach tasted absolutely awful.

   ___7. Andrew studied his reflection in the mirror and decorated his face with a magic marker.

Possible Sentences Form

1. **Write the key concepts here:**

_____   _____   _____   _____

_____   _____   _____   _____

_____   _____   _____   _____

_____   _____   _____   _____

2. **Possible Sentences –Postreading reaction (T, F, DK–Don't Know)**

1._____
2_____
3._____
4._____
5._____
6._____
7._____
8._____
9._____
10.____

3. **Modified Sentences**

1._____

_____

2._____

_____

3._____

_____

4._____

_____

5._____

_____

6._____

_____

7._____

_____

8._____

_____

9._____

_____

10._____

_____

RAFT

Objective: To help students structure writing assignments enabling them to learn more about content material as well as learning about writing for specific audiences.

Rationale/Description: A system to help students understand their role as a writer, the audience they will address, the varied formats for writing and the expected content. Almost all RAFT writing assignments are written from a viewpoint different from the student's, to another audience rather than the teacher, and in a form different from the ordinary theme.

Intended for: Upper elementary level, intermediate and above.

Procedures:

Explication

    Step One: Explain to the students how all writers have to consider various aspects before every writing assignment including role, audience, format, and topic. Tell them that they are going to structure their writing around these elements. (It is helpful to display these elements on chart paper or bulletin board for future reference.)

    R - *Role of the writer* Who or what are you? (A scientist, a car, George Washington?)
    A - *Audience* To whom is this written? (A friend, a police officer, a teacher?)
    F - *Format* What kind of form will it take? (A journal entry, a letter, a memo?)
    T - *Topic plus a strong verb* Persuade a company to hire you, demand for fair treatment as a slave, plead for a ride on a rocket ship.

    Step Two: Display a completed RAFT example (such as the one that follows) on the overhead and discuss the key elements as a class.

Modeling/Demonstration

    Step Three: Then "think aloud" another sample RAFT exercise with the aid of the class. Brainstorm additional topic ideas and write down the suggestions listing roles, audiences, formats, and strong verbs associated with each topic.

    Step Four: Assign students to small, heterogeneous groups of four or five or pairs and have them "put their heads together" to write about a chosen topic with one RAFT assignment between them.

Guided Practice

    Step Five: Circulate among the groups to provide assistance as needed. Then have the groups share their completed assignments with the class.

Step Six: After students become more proficient in developing this style of writing, have them generate RAFT assignments of their own based on current topics studied in class.

Santa, C. M. (1988). *Content reading including study systems: Reading, writing and studying across the curriculum.* Dubuque, IA: Kendall/Hunt Pub. Co.

RAFT
Fourth-grade Math (Division/Sharing)

R **Math Operation (Division)**
A **Classmates**
F **Speech or Letter**
T **Convince audience that division has many important daily uses.**

Dear Students,

My name is Division, and I am a mathematical operation that can help you in many ways. Sadly, sometimes students seem afraid of me, or think that I am too confusing to be useful. But if you give me a chance, you will see that I can save you valuable time, and maybe even help you keep your friends!

For example, imagine that you and your two best friends just ordered a pizza for lunch. The pizza is cut into 12 slices, and you are wondering just how to decide how many slices of pizza you and you friends should eat. You want to be fair to everyone, but you aren't sure how many slices each of you should get. You could count out the slices one-by-one, but the pizza would be cold before you finished! So to solve your problem, you divide.

You have 12 slices of pizza, right? And two friends, plus you, equals three people to eat the pizza. If you divide 12 by three, the answer you get is four. So that's it: You and each of your friends is allowed to eat four slices of hot, delicious pizza! And you figured it out in no time at all!

So you see, division can be a very helpful tool. I can help you solve many problems: I could tell you how 5 dogs could share 17 dog treats, or how many 8-person soccer teams could be made of a class of 24 students. Just give me a try—Division can be lots of fun, and as you can see, I can also be very useful!

Your friend,

Division

RAFT Writing Strategy

Name_____Partner(s)_____

1. Tell the following about your chosen RAFT writing assignment:

R: *Role of the writer* (Who or what are you?)_____

A: *Audience* (To whom is this written? A friend, a police officer, a teacher?)
_____

F: *Format* What kind of form will it take? A journal entry, a letter, a memo?)
_____

T: *Topic: (*Persuade a company to hire you, demand for fair treatment as a slave, plead for a ride on a rocket ship) _____

2. Use the space below to compose your idea.

Paired Reading for Fluency

Objective: To help students improve their smoothness of reading while simultaneously reinforcing key concepts.

Rationale/Description: In order to ensure that the reading ability of beginning or struggling readers improves, it is necessary to give them ample opportunities throughout the day to practice fluency. Fluency refers to smoothness of reading, the ability to read material with few interruptions due to inadequate word attack or word recognition problems. Paired reading is one strategy which is designed to help students develop reading fluency by giving them practice with peers. *For many students, fluency practice should take place at least once a day and should last approximately 15 to 20 minutes.*

Intended for: Elementary, middle, secondary and students who need additional support.

Procedures:

Preparation Phase

> **Step One:** Make sure that materials are available to practice fluency. These passages or books should be short, 25; 50-100 words, depending on the ability level of the students. They should also be passages that pose no comprehension problems for the students, since the purpose of the assignment is to practice fluency. Short workbook segments or tradebook excerpts written at low levels are usually appropriate. Passages that are related to the content under study are especially useful to reinforce the learning of key concepts while simultaneously practicing reading skills.

> **Step Two:** Pre-assign the struggling or beginning readers to pairs, making certain that the students are sufficiently similar in ability that they can mutually benefit from peer instruction. Tell them that the purpose of this assignment is to help them become better readers and that improving the ability to read, as with any sport or activity, requires that they practice each day.

> **Step Three:** Students first read their passages silently and then decide who will practice reading first. Students alternate the roles of reader and listener throughout the practice session.

> **Step Four:** When asked to serve as reader, the student reads the passage aloud to the partner three different times. The partner can assist with pronunciation and meaning if needed. Then the reader engages in a self-evaluation answering the question, "How well did you read?" When asked to serve as the listener, the

student listens to the partner's reading and then notes how the reading improved on the evaluation form. *Note that the only opportunity for partners to evaluate one another requires a positive response, not a negative one.*

Step Five: After the third reading, the students switch roles and follow step 3 again. Teachers should circulate among the dyads to provide assistance, take notes (either mental or written) and model effective fluent reading for the students.

Adapted from Koskinen, P. S. & Blum, I. H. (1986) Paired repeated reading: A classroom strategy for developing fluent reading. *The Reading Teacher, 40*(1), 70-75.

Partner Reading Assessment

Name_____ Partner _____

Date _____ We read _____

Reading #1
How well did you read?   **Score!!**   **Good!**   **OK**   **Try Again**

Reading #2
How well did you read

Reading #3
How well did you read?

How did your partner's reading improve?

    Read more smoothly   _____

    Knew more words   _____

    Read with more expression   _____

Tell your partner one thing that was better about his or her reading _____

_____

_____

_____

Probable Passages

Objective: To reinforce students' knowledge and understanding by using key vocabulary, prediction and writing.

Rationale/Description: In Probable Passages, students use their knowledge of how stories are structured, as well as their inferencing abilities, to predict the content of selections to be read. Six major story grammar elements are typically found in stories in our western culture: 1) setting (introduction of characters, time and location); 2) beginning (a precipitating event); 3) reaction (main character's responses to the beginning or the formation of a goal); 4) attempt (plan to reach a goal); 5) outcome (success or failure of attempt); and 6) ending (long range consequences). Students use key concepts from a selection in a class constructed passage, reflecting their predictions about the story. This collaborative approach to composition models the writing process for less proficient writers and allows the teacher to emphasize vocabulary, comprehension and writing within a single lesson.

Intended for: Elementary, intermediate, middle and secondary level students and students who need additional support.

Procedures:

Preparation stage

> **Step One:** Analyze the selection for the most significant concepts, terms or names that reflect the key ideas/events and present these on the board or an overhead projector.

> **Step Two:** Display the blank frame which lists the story structure elements at the top and the incomplete probable passage at the bottom on the overhead projector. (Note these elements can be changed to coordinate with story type.)

Prereading Stage

> **Step Three:** Tell the students that they are going to be engaged in a strategy to help them use the key vocabulary of a story to predict what the story is probably about. Tell them this strategy is designed to help them improve their vocabulary, comprehension and writing skills.

> **Step Four:** After reading the words with the students, tell the class to use the words to mentally construct a story line. Then, as a class, "slot" the words in the appropriate categories. Tell them that some words may fit in more than one category and that they can fill in with other words not listed that their background knowledge suggests may be feasible. (See words in quotation marks in the sample lesson.)

Step Five: Direct the class's attention to each line of the story frame and have them use the words to develop a logical, probable passage.

Reading Stage

Step Six: Have the students read the selection individually or in pairs with their predicted story lines in mind.

Postreading Stage

Step Eight: After reading and discussing the story, have the class make the necessary changes on the categorized word frame.

Step Nine: Have the class modify the probable passage to reflect the actual events of the selection.

Optional Step: After more than one experience with this strategy as a class, students can work in small groups or pairs to construct probable and actual passages for other stories. They can share their probable passages with other groups to note the range of alternatives.

Wood, K. D. (1984) Probable passages: A writing strategy. *The Reading Teacher*, February, 496-499.

Sample Key Concept Frame

Setting	Character(s)	Problem	Problem/ Solution	Ending
doughnut shop bakery	Tomas " a little boy" Mr. Tucker "owner of shop"	whirr! buzz! clunk! machine flour huge start button	bank loan invented customer money	delicious jelly-cinnamon-honey doughnut

Sample Probable Passage

The story takes place <u>in a doughnut shop</u>. <u>Mr. Tucker</u> is a character in the story who <u>owns the store</u>. A problem occurs when <u>Tomas, a little boy, pushes the start-button</u>. After that, <u>the machines goes whirr, buzz and clunk and a huge doughnut pops out</u>. Next, <u>a customer comes in</u>. The problem is solved <u>when they are given a bank loan and Mr. Tucker and Tomas invent a way to stop the machine</u>. The story ends when <u>Tomas eats a delicious jelly-cinnamon-honey doughnut</u>.

Actual Passage After Reading

The story takes place <u>in a doughnut shop</u>. <u>Tomas</u> is the character who <u>invented the jelly-cinnamon-honey doughnut. Mr. Tucker is the owner of the store</u>. A problem occurs when <u>Tomas pushes the start-button and can't figure out how to stop the machine</u>. After that, <u>he pushes all the buttons together, the machine goes whirr, buzz and clunk and a huge, jelly-cinnamon-honey doughnut pops out</u>. Next, <u>Mr. Redstone, a customer, comes in and buys all the doughnuts</u>. The problem is solved <u>when customers come from all around to buy the doughnuts and Mr. Tucker doesn't have to take out a bank loan.</u> The story ends when <u>Mr. Tucker lets Tomas have a free jelly-cinnamon-honey doughnut every day.</u>

Blank Concept Frame

Setting	Character(s)	Problem	Problem/ Solution	Ending

Blank Passage Form

The story takes place _____ .

_____ is a character in the story who _____

_____ . A problem occurs when

_____ .

After that, _____

_____ .

Next, _____

_____

The problem is solved when _____

_____ .

The story ends _____

_____

Think Pair Share

Objective: To give students ample time to formulate an answer and undertake a learning task that involves discussion and sharing with a partner and the whole class.

Rationale/Description: Think pair share is a discussion strategy in which students think individually and share with classmates how to answer a question, solve a problem or undertake a learning task. It is a preferred alternative to calling on individual students randomly in a class and expecting them to answer on the spot. The act of discussing their thinking with a partner serves a kind of "dress rehearsal" before they are asked to "go public" with their responses in front of the class. It is also useful to engage in a "think pair share" activity when students are not responding to a question. The act of discussing an answer with a partner serves to maximize participation, focus their attention and engage them in the learning task.

Intended for: Elementary, intermediate, middle and secondary and students who need additional support.

Procedures:

Step One: Discuss the purpose of the collaborative strategy as a discussion starter, a means of stimulating their thinking and prior knowledge on a topic. One useful option is to display the steps of the strategy on a poster in the room to cue each phrase along the way.

Step Two: Pose a question or a problem then give the students ample time to think about their responses and jot them down on their think pair share think sheet.

Step Three: Then, have them pair up with a pre-assigned partner or someone seated nearby to discuss their thinking, writing down their responses on the form.

Step Four: Next, tell the students to share their thinking with the entire class. Newly learned answers and additional responses can be written on the "think sheet" for future referral.

Kagan, S. (1994). *Cooperative learning.* San Juan Capistrano, CA: Kagan Cooperative Learning.

Think Pair Share "Think Sheet"

Name_____ Partner_____

1. By yourself think about_____.
   Write notes here.

2. Share your thinking with a partner. Write your shared notes here.

3. Share your ideas with the class. Write down some new things you have
   learned.

Double Entry Journal

Objective: To help students reflect on and process new information from both print and nonprint sources.

Rationale/Description: The Double Entry Journal, useful for both expository and narrative material, is also called the dialectic, dialogue or two column journal. It is a system of note-taking in which the learner essentially engages in a discussion with the author, reflecting about and questioning specific information. Notes about the text or viewed material are written in the left hand side of the paper under the "What the Author Said" section and notes on the notes, the learner's personal responses are written under the "What You Say" section.

Intended for: Elementary, Intermediate, Middle and Secondary

Procedures:

Modeling/Demonstration Phase

Step One: Display the blank form on an overhead projector and explain to the students that they will learn a way to take notes that involves talking with the author and asking questions, making analogies, and expressing thoughts and reactions to the content or events.

Step Two: Display either the narrative or expository example and walk the students through the some of the sample questions and comments.

Step Three: Use a sample passage and "talk aloud" some possible responses, enlisting the aid of the class in the process.

Guided Practice Phase

Step Four: Use another sample passage and divide the class into heterogeneous groups or pairs to engage in the double entry journal process. Circulate among the groups to provide assistance.

Step Five: Have the groups share their responses with the entire class. Direct the students' attention to the fact that their responses in the "What the Author Said" portion are often very similar, but in the "What you say" section, the responses are more personal and individual.

Independent Practice Phase

Step Six: Allow the students to work in pairs or individually to try out the procedure independently.

Application Phase

Step Seven: Have the students apply the note-taking procedure to other subjects as well.

Schatzberg-Smith, K. (1989). Dialectic notes: Learner-driven interaction with text. Language Connections: A Newsletter of the Reading/Communications Resource Center. Hempstead, NY: Hofstra University.

Sample Double Entry Journal with Fiction
The Gunnywolf

Notes	Notes on Notes
What the Author Said	**What You Say**
Setting, Time, Place	**Questions you want to ask**
The deep dark woods	*Why would she take a chance going in the dark woods with a wolf?*
Main Characters (name, role, traits)	
Little Girl liked to pick flowers ***The Gunnywolf liked to scare people***	**Statements that start with "but or "however"**
Main events (plot, problem/conflict, Building action, Climax, resolution)	***On page 98, it says "but one day she saw a flower in the*** woods *and forgot all about the wolf—that's why she went deeper in the woods*
Everytime she sings her song, it puts the wolf to sleep	
Theme (What is the author trying to get you to think about?)	**Consequences (What might the characters do next if the story continues?)**
Sometimes we can control our fears more than we think	*I think the wolf and little girl **will be friends as long as she** keeps on singing*
Quotable quotes	**Experiences you have had or stories that are similar**
Un-ka-cha, pit-a-pat *"Sing that good, sweet song song again."*	*This reminds me of Little Red Riding Hood and Lon Po Po*
	Other themes
	It's still not a good idea to walk in the woods alone
	Evaluation (Would you Encourage a friend to read This? Explain.)
	Yes, it was fun to read the crazy words and it had a happy ending

Sample Double Entry Journal for Non-Fiction

<u>Notes</u>	<u>Notes on Notes</u>
What the Author Said	**What You Say**
Author's main points	Questions you want to ask
Important details	Arguments (statements that start with "but" or "however")
Quotable quotes	Suggestions, etc. (Ideas the author should have discussed, but didn't)
Author's conclusions	Other knowledge or experience you have had on the topic
Details	Evaluation (Reasons you agree or disagree with the author)
	Consequences (Results or effects of the author's ideas)

Sample Double Entry Journal for Non-Fiction

Notes	Notes on Notes
What the Author Said	**What You Say**

Reader Response Form

Objective: To manage and organize the self-selected reading program in a classroom.

Rationale/Description: An aim of every literacy teacher is to provide daily opportunities for independent reading in material students have chosen themselves. One of the most difficult demands of this objective is how to manage and maintain adequate records on children's choices. The Reader Response Form provides a means of keeping track of students' reading choices as well as a way in which they respond to the reading. However, the form can be used in conjunction with any reading requirements—assigned or self-selected.

Intended for: Elementary, intermediate, middle, and secondary students.

Procedures:

Step One: After promoting the benefits of your classroom or schoolwide independent reading program, introduce the form by passing out copies to students and/or displaying a copy on the overhead projector. Explain to the students that this form will help them organize their reading selections and receive credit for their efforts.

Step Two: Each day or week, show examples and model the many ways students can respond to their reading.

Step Three: Place the forms near the book displays or reading corner where they are easily accessible to the students.

Step Four: One option is to have students select the way they want to respond to a self-selected book and use the form to record their responses. Another option is to assign a reading selection (from a basal anthology, for example) and allow students to choose the way they want to respond.

Step Five: Students may be asked to share their books and methods of responding in small groups.

Step Six: The completed forms may be included in students' portfolios and shared with parents.

Wood, K.D. (1994). *Practical strategies for improving instruction.* Columbus, OH: National Middle School Association.

Reader Response Form

Name _____ Class _____ Date _____

Title of Book _____

Author _____

I chose this book because _____

Number of pages: _____

I read the entire book ___ Yes   ___ No

I read the book   ___ at home   ___ at school

                         ___ both

Reaction to the book:				
1	**2**	**3**	**4**	**5**
Disliked The book		The book was OK		Really liked the book

Choose the way you want to respond to this book. Attach your response to this form.

Newspaper article, advertisement

Timeline of major events

Take a position on an issue in the book

Book jacket, poster, blurb

My favorite part(s) is/are…

My favorite character(s) is/are…

Write a letter to a friend about the book

Design a book jacket

Write a skit, play, song, poem

Describe an experience from the perspective of a character or thing in the book

Talk show interview with _____

If I could change one thing about the book it would be…

After reading this book, I learned…

Book review

Book conference with teacher

Conduct a book-talk for the class or group

This book reminded of…

I was puzzled by…

Write in my journal (free response)

Make a collage or mobile

Other _____

Wood, K.D. (2000). *Literacy strategies across the subject areas*. Boston: Allyn & Bacon Publishing Co.

Imagine, Elaborate, Predict and Confirm (IEPC)

Objective: To encourage students to use visual imagery as a means of enriching their understanding of information which is viewed, listened to or read.

Rationale/Description: IEPC is a strategy to help students increase their understanding and recall by using visual imagery to predict events in a selection. It begins by modeling for students how to imagine a scene, add details and then use their thinking to predict a possible story line. After reading, students return to confirm or disconfirm their original predictions. The specific components of IEPC are:

  ▸ **Imagine:** Close your eyes and try to imagine the scene. Share your thinking with a partner and the whole class.
  ▸ **Elaborate:** Think of details surrounding the scene in your head. How do you think the characters feel? What are similar experiences? Describe the scene. What do you see, feel, hear, smell?
  ▸ **Predict:** Use what you have imagined in your head to predict what might happen in the story (characters, events, setting, etc.)
  ▸ **Confirm:** During and after reading the selection, think about your original predictions. Were they true, false or were they not explained in the passage. Modify your predictions to coordinate with the actual selection.

Intended for: Elementary, middle, secondary.

Procedures:

Modeling Phase

Step One: Decide upon an appropriate tradebook, basal selection or passage with content appropriate for developing imagery.

Step Two: Display the IEPC blank form on the overhead projector and tell the students that they are going to engage in a strategy designed to encourage them to use their imaginations to create pictures of what they see in their mind. Tell them that making pictures or images before, during and after reading will help them understand and remember what they read.

Step Three: Use the transparency to point out and explain the four phases of IEPC using language appropriate to their ability levels.

Prereading Stage

Step Four: Tell the students that they are going to read/hear a selection. Begin with the imagine phase and ask the students to join you in closing their eyes and imagining everything they can about the selection to be read. This may be based upon the cover of a book, a title or a topic. Encourage the students to use sensory experiences by imagining feelings, taste, smell, sight and surroundings.

Step Five: Talk aloud your thinking and then ask the class if they have anything to add. Write the responses in the "I" column on the form.

Step Six: Model for the students how to use their visual images and add details, anecdotes, prior experiences, sensory information, etc. and jot this information in the "E" column.

Step Seven: Talk aloud at least one sample prediction, based upon prior visual images and encourage the students to do the same. Write these responses in the "P" column.

Reading Stage
Step Eight: Have students read/listen to the selection(or segment) with these predictions in mind.

Postreading Stage
Step Nine: After reading, return to the transparency and, using a different color marker, modify the original predictions to coordination with the newly learned information.

Wood, K. D. & Douville, P. (1999) Imagine, Elaborate, Predict and Confirm (IEPC): Using visual imagery to enhance comprehension. Presentation for the National Reading Conference. Orlando, Florida.

Imagine, Elaborate, Predict, and Confirm (IEPC)

Sample student responses before and after reading *A Snake in the House*, by Faith McNulty (illustrated by Ted Rand).

I	E	P	C
The Snake is slimy, and it slithers and flicks its tongue. I feel nervous and scared I see the snake moving quickly across the floor.	The snake's scales are slimy, and its dark cold eyes stare at me. The snake is crawling through the house, and I am afraid it will bite me. The snake slithers quickly across the floor as it searches for something to eat.	The snake and the cat will fight, and the snake will bite the cat in the neck. Someone will catch the snake and take it outside.	The snake searches the house for food and a way to escape. The cat tries to catch the snake, but the snake gets away. The snake crawls into a basket and the boy carries it outside. Finally, the boy grabs the snake and sets it free. The snake felt warm, dry, and alive. It has a powerful body. It crawls quickly through the grass toward its home.

Imagine, Elaborate, Predict, and Confirm (IEPC)
Sample student responses

I	E	P	C
Close your eyes and imagine the scene, character, events. What do you see, feel, hear, smell? Share your thinking with a partner.	Elaborate—tell/describe/give details of what you "see" in your mind.	Use these ideas to make some predictions/guesses about the passages to be read.	Read to confirm or change your predictions about the passage.
Wolf!	I see a big brownish-black wolf with his teeth showing. He is growling and licking his lips. He's hungry and pacing back and forth. I see a storybook wolf who ends up being nice to everyone.	I predict he will try to attack some little animals or people. Hunters will probably have to go after him. Maybe he'll get something to eat and calm down.	He looks like a wolf but he goes to school, wears glasses, and reads. He starts off being mean but the duck, pig, and cow ignore him since they are reading. He tries to scare the animals by howling and jumping at them. Only the chickens and rabbits run away. He goes to school and learns to read. He does calm down when he learns to read.

Imagine, Elaborate, Predict, and Confirm (IEPC)

Blank Form

I	E	P	C
Close your eyes and imagine the scene, character, events. What do you see, feel, hear, smell? Share your thinking with a partner.	Elaborate— tell/describe/give details of what you "see" in your mind.	Use these ideas to make some predictions/guesses about the passages to be read.	Read to confirm or change your predictions about the passage.

Story Frames

Objective: To help focus students' writing in response to reading and to enhance comprehension.

Rationale/Description: Story frames is a sequence of spaces connected by key language elements to help students focus their writing. The purpose of story frames is threefold: 1) to provide a framework to guide students' understanding and responding; 2) to give a structured format to follow for engaging in a writing activity; and 3) to help students develop independent comprehension strategies.

Intended for: Elementary, intermediate, middle and secondary level students, particularly beginning readers and writers and students who need additional support.

Procedures:

Modeling Stage (Whole Class)

Step One: Use the blank form included here and display it on an overhead projector. Ask the students if they have ever had problems deciding what to write about when asked to summarize a selection. Explain to the students that this frame, like the frame of a new house, will allow them to fill the blanks with information from the selection just read.

Step Two: With the students following along, read aloud the problem-solution frame and explain that many stories they read have a situation where a problem occurs that must be solved by a character who takes action.

Step Three: Read a story aloud that follows the problem-solution theme and together with the class fill in the frame. It may be necessary for the teacher to "think-aloud" a few examples to model the process.

Step Four: Have students volunteer to read the frame orally.

Guided Practice (Small group, pairs)

Step Five: Introduce a story which students may read silently, orally in pairs or a combination of both.

Step Six: After the reading and discussing of the story, have the students work in pairs (or groups) to produce one common frame between the dyads.

Step Seven: Have students share their frames with others to determine how their composition "sounds." Optional buddy system editing can be employed here.

Step Eight: Repeat the process using other frame formats as deemed necessary.

Independent Practice

Step Nine: After modeling and practicing various frames, blank frames can be made available in the reading corner.

Step Ten: Students can choose their own story and complete the appropriate frame.

Step Eleven: Students may be asked to share and edit their frames with a partner before turning it in for credit.

Step Twelve: When deemed appropriate, allow students to write summaries first in pairs and then on their own without the aid of a partner or a frame.

Fowler, G. (1982) Developing comprehension skills in primary students through the use of story frames. *The Reading Teacher*, 36, 2, November.

Important Idea or Plot Frame

The Three Little Pigs

In this story, a problem begins when ___ three pigs decide to build houses made of three different things ___.

After that, ___ a big, bad wolf comes along to eat them ___.

Next, ___ the wolf blows down the house made of straw and eats the pig who lives inside ___.

Then, ___ the wolf blows down the house made of sticks and eats the pig who lives there ___.

The problem is solved when ___ the wolf tries to blow down the house made of bricks, but he can't do it ___.

The story ends when ___ the wolf dies from trying so hard to blow down the brick house ___.

Important Idea or Plot Frame

In this story, a problem begins when _____

_____

_____. After that,

_____

Next _____

_____

_____. Then,

_____

_____

_____.

The problem is solved when _____

_____

_____

_____

_____The story ends

when_____

_____

_____

_____.

Setting Frame

This story takes place _____

_____

_____.

I know this because the author uses the words _____

_____

_____.

Other clues that show when and where the story takes place are _____

_____

_____

_____.

Character Analysis Frame

In the story _____

by _____ the major character is

_____ who is _____

_____

_____.

Another main character is _____.

The problem that the major character faces is that _____

_____

_____The story ends with _____

_____

_____

_____.

The lesson I learned from reading this story was that _____

_____

_____

_____

Character Comparison Frame

_____ and _____
       (character's name)   (character's name)

are two characters in our story, _____
                                            (title)

_____.

_____ is _____
       (character's name)   (trait)

_____while _____
                                        (other character)

is _____
                                (trait)

_____.

For instance, _____ tries to _____
                     (character)

and _____ tries to _____
           (other character)

_____.

_____ learn(s) a lesson when _____
       (character)

_____.

Field Trip Writing Frame

Objective: To give students additional practice in writing and to help direct their attention on major concepts.

Rationale/Objective: Like story frames described previously, the Field Trip Writing Frame is a sequence of spaces connected by key language elements to help students focus their writing. This frame also enables teachers to "smuggle" writing into field trips in a non-threatening, enjoyable manner. The frame itself can be modified to include language elements that reflect the major topics under study.

Intended for: Elementary, intermediate, middle and secondary students and students for whom additional support is needed.

Procedures:

Model/Demonstrate

Step One: Display the blank form included here on an overhead projector and explain to the class that this frame is designed to help them summarize important experiences on the field trip they are about to take. NOTE: Teachers may find it helpful, but not always necessary, to introduce the field trip writing frame after modeling and practice of story frames.

Step Two: In order to model and demonstrate its use, the teacher and students may take a brief tour of the school or surroundings, with the frame elements in mind. Then together they can fill in the frame by noting what was observed or experienced. The teacher may choose to "think aloud" the first few sentences, if needed.

Step Three: Before going on the actual field trip, remind the class that they will be summarizing the event by describing their experiences on the writing frame. Students can be assigned a partner, particularly if extra support is needed, or they can work alone to produce their recollection of what occurred on the trip and what they learned in the process.

Step Four: Students may be asked to illustrate their frames to coordinate with what was observed on the trip.

Step Five: Have students proofread their frames with a partner or small group.

Step Six: Students may be asked to volunteer to read their frames orally to partners or the class.

Step Seven: Display the completed frames and illustrations in the classroom.

Field Trip Frame

Name __Alex Blevins__   Partner __Derek Jacobs__

Yesterday I went to _____Pleasant Prairie Pioneer Settlement_ with my class. The first thing I saw ___was the one-room___ _schoolhouse_ . Next, __we saw the__ _blacksmith shop_ . Then, ___we___ _walked through a pioneer home._ After that, ___we went into the_ _barn and saw a cow being milked_ . Then, _our last stop was_ _the trading post, where I bought a rabbit's fur and a round metal_ _ball that was used as a bullet_ . I also ___learned_ that children _had_ to do many chores before and after school . If we go back again, I __would ask the lady if I could help her make a candle__ .

Field Trip Frame

Name _____   Partner_____

Yesterday I went to _____

_____ with my class.

The first thing I _____

_____

_____. Next _____

_____

_____. Then, _____

_____

_____

_____. After that, _____

_____

_____

_____. Then, _____

_____

_____. Because of this trip, I learned _____

_____

_____. I also learned _____

_____.

If we go back again, I _____

_____

_____

_____

Story Impressions

Objective: To reinforce students' vocabulary knowledge, predictive abilities, comprehension and writing performance.

Rationale/Description: Story impressions is a writing strategy designed for the pre-reading stage of the instructional lesson. It is particularly appropriate for narrative material because key phrases or words are pulled from a selection and presented in exactly the same order in which they appeared in the actual story. Students use these key terms to predict the story line before reading, thereby drawing upon their pre-existing knowledge of how stories are structured.

Intended for: Elementary, intermediate, middle, secondary.

Procedures:

Prereading Phase

Step One: The teacher begins by selecting key phrases from the story/ selection to be read, making certain that these key phrases represent the action, theme, main concepts of the story.

Step Two: These phrases should be presented in *the order in which they appear in the story.* The blank form included here may be converted to a transparency and the terms inserted on the lines in part one to be displayed on an overhead projector.

Step Three: Read the phrases aloud to the students and have them repeat each phrase. Discuss and clarify any terms, concepts as necessary. Encourage the students to imagine and visualize the events and characters.

Step Four: Tell the students that they are to use these key phrases to predict a possible story line. Remind them that the key phrases are presented in order.

Step Five: The prediction phase may be done as a whole class or students may be grouped heterogeneously with four to five members. The teacher can circulate to listen in, provide assistance and monitor participation.

Step Six: Ask the groups to volunteer their predicted story lines.

Reading Phase

Step Seven: Have students read the story, paying attention to the key phrases introduced and how they contribute to the plot. Discuss and clarify the phrases/terms with information in the story.

Postreading Phase

Step Eight: An optional step is to have the students return to the key phrases and reconstruct another passage to coordinate with the actual events of the story. This may be done as a whole class or in groups and may be done orally or in written form, depending upon time constraints.

McGinley, W. J. & Denner, P. R. (1987). A prereading/writing activity. *Journal of Reading 31*, 248-253.

Story Impressions: *Uncle Jed's Barbershop* by Margaree King Mitchell

Jedediah Johnson/favorite uncle → Traveling black barber
←

Going to own barbershop → Someday
←

Lived in South → People were poor
←

Niece gets sick → Hospital segregated
←

$300.00 for operation → Found Uncle Jed
←

Barbershop delayed → Great Depression
←

Cut hair for food → 79th birthday
←

Barbershop → Taught me to dream

I had a favorite uncle named Jedediah Johnson. He was a traveling black barber and he loved to cut people's hair. (Sara) He knew that someday he was going to have his own barbershop and then he would not have to travel from town to town cutting hair. (Rodnico) We all lived in the South and we were all very poor. One day I got very sick and had to go to the hospital. The hospital was segregated and the doctor wouldn't see me. (Queint) Finally the doctor saw me and he said it would cost $300 for the operation. Well we didn't have that kind of money because we were poor. We had to find Uncle Jed. (Sara) Uncle Jed had to delay his barbershop because he didn't have any money either because it was the Great Depression. He gave me the money for the operation, but it left him broke. (Rodnico) He was so poor after he gave me the money that he had to cut hair just to get food. (Queint) Finally on his 79th birthday we bought him a barbershop for a present. Uncle Jed taught me to dream. (Sara)

Reprinted from Wood, K.D. & Nichols, W. D. (2000). Helping struggling learners read and write. In K.D. Wood & T. S. Dickinson. *Promoting Literacy in grades 4 – 9.* Boston: Allyn & Bacon.

Story Impressions Form

Part 1: Predict how the terms below might be used in the selection to be read.

_____   _____   _____

_____   _____   _____

_____   _____   _____

_____   _____   _____

Part 2: Write your predicted passage in the space below.

Part 3: Read the selection and use the terms again in another passage.